Praise for *Spellbook fo...*

"Reverent, irreverent, honest, erotic, and ethereal, these tknines for ... ...
are essential to forming a new language and imagination to make the world anew. This is
heartbreaking, authentic poetry full of introspection. And it's necessary—now."

—Michael W. Twitty, author of *The Cooking Gene*

"In Fox's dazzling confessional verse, Jewish, pagan, and queer identities mingle without
apology. This book of spells is also a book of longing, an act of inscribing the poet's
long-submerged but vital sense of self. Here, we do not wait for the Shabbat Bride to
knock—she is always and already with us."

—AJ Odasso, author of *The Sting of It* and *The Pursued and the Pursuing*

"To read Fox's work is to enter an honest and open exploration of the most intimate
parts of ourselves and the knowledge—and beauty—that blooms there. From spiritual
longing to longing for a friendship to become something deeper to a glorious exploration
of Sappho's vocabulary of flowers, these stunning poems travel the length of the rainbowed arc connecting all who dare to be who they truly are. These poems speak not just
to the necessity of living in full honesty but also its beauty, in which even sorrow has its
place: '*after all, / you might never have seen / the rainbows crowding your heart / without
the bleak help of / clouds.*'"

—Emma Bolden, author of *The Tiger and the Cage: A Memoir of a Body in Crisis*

"The poems of *Spellbook for the Sabbath Queen* by Elisheva Fox are oceanic—not only
in the sense of their emotional generosity, but in how they carry the ocean in their being: wave-crashing, salt-aired, at times iridescent. While reckoning with the weight of
religious forms and the place of queer desire in personal history, the speaker locates their
own blessing in the confession: 'but as it turns out, / the heart is a buoyant thing.' How
they lift the reader with their ocean magic, these poems. How they make space for queer
love and witchery inside the living frameworks of Judaism, parenthood, and marriage."

—Han VanderHart, author of *What Pecan Light*

"Elisheva Fox's debut collection, *Spellbook for the Sabbath Queen*, is a song that wakes us
in the darkness. Full of heartache and yearning, these poems of faith and family and desire
dive like large birds beneath oil slick rainbows on the Gulf, fishing for the forbidden. The
speaker's ribs crack under the stress of blooming violets, while 'our plumbing [is] ruptured'
and we do our best not to drown. Fox's poems are haunting in their tenderness, a 'spotted
fawn' that 'trembles in the long grass,' but are not content to stay hidden. Her mourning
for what has yet to be claimed is counterbalanced by the gleam of the wolf's smile after
biting a husband's hand or the witch that asks us to stop wasting her time. Fox suggests
we are all within the curve of aorta and spray of ventricles, impatient for transformation."

—Jared Beloff, author of *Who Will Cradle Your Head*

spellbook for the sabbath queen.

ELISHEVA FOX

POEMS

spellbook for the sabbath queen.

BELLE
POINT
PRESS

Fort Smith, Arkansas

SPELLBOOK FOR THE SABBATH QUEEN.

© 2023 Elisheva Fox

Cover image: *Portrait of an unknown woman*
(*Portret van een onbekende vrouw*) (1913),
Samuel Jessurun de Mesquita.
Original from The Rijksmuseum, via rawpixel.

Edited by Casie Dodd
Design & typography by Belle Point Press

Belle Point Press, LLC
Fort Smith, Arkansas
bellepointpress.com
editor@bellepointpress.com

Find Belle Point Press
on Facebook,
Twitter (@BellePointPress),
and Instagram (@bellepointpress)

Printed in the United States of America

27 26 25 24 23   1 2 3 4 5

Library of Congress Control Number: 2023931719

ISBN: 978-1-960215-00-0

SSQ/BPP11

CONTENTS

keter.

what a loss,
when you crowd a page
with black and unlit letters—

think on all the things
that might have bloomed

if you had not hurried.

0: the fool.

scientists say:
the arctic shelves
are on the verge of crumbling.

one degree, two degrees—
that's all it takes for the ice
to lose its grip on
itself.

do you think glaciers know
that when the spidercracks
start   the end is beginning?

did i know that when you
looked at me with violence
in your curled fingers that
the end was beginning?

maybe.

avinu malkeinu, 5781.

this year we were not permitted
to flock in our synagogue pews,
under the tessellated light of
stained glass.

this year we were not permitted
to sway the way oaks beg
a hurricane wind for mercy.

still, the cantor sings:

avinu malkeinu.

our father, our king.
are you listening,
this year?
were you ever listening?

i know six million ghosts
who probably asked that question,
and who are far more deserving
of an answer.

i just don't understand
why a man who won't
eat pigs or shellfish because you
said not to—

why will that man
stroke my elbow,
      slip his thumb
            under the sleeve of my dress,
suggest that i should

masturbate in his shower

as my children, his son's children,
his grandchildren,
draw a dusty galaxy
of chalk planets
outside on the sidewalk?

         is that kosher?

this year,

         is that permitted?

selkie.

i remember when we sprinkled
my uncle
across the gray green gulf.

i remember my grandmother
was a pallid wash of foamy white,
bent in a way she never was again
until the shabbat before she died.

i remember my father crying.

i remember my mother whispering,
hissing under her breath about
lifestyle choices.

when the waves tilted just so—
under my uncle's ashes,
i could see rainbows.

for so long,
i chose to style a life underwater,
i chose to live flounder flat and tasteless,
i chose to ignore the insistent siren song
of my wants.

but as it turns out,
the heart is a buoyant thing,
and a patient thing,
and you cannot stay
beneath the murky sea forever.

one day, you will
break the surface
gasping, flashing,
slick with a thousand colors.

kelp.

a thunderstorm
slipped over the beach
and out to sea.

gray rain sluiced down
venous trees

and gray ocean waves
stretched up

as though they might meet
and kiss
in the middle of the sky,

two halves
of one moon touched heart
broken
by the sun.

after a downpour—
after the dark and the thunder—
the sand is always
packed firm,

more determined to hold
onto the imprint
of everything that has passed

light loops of gull feet,
cursive scuttles from carapaced crabs,
the careful semicolon from
a woman's sandal.

and everywhere,
over the white glass amnion,
bundles of curly seaweed
perfume the breeze
with salt.

marrow.

florida beach water
is a disorienting blue.

i am a child of
the texas gulf,
gray and slick
with iridescent oil.

but here the waves
curl turquoise
and tame at
my feet.

i scoop bone white   sand
into new parapets
that crumble
almost instantly.

my children
laugh and laugh
as ocean foam
wreaths their knees.

hands roped together,
saltwater taffy women
walk past us—
they wave
to my husband,
to me.

what a thing
it would be
to swell like the tide,
to flash as clear
as the water here,

so that these
women could see
the riot of violets
splitting my ribs,
the rainbow arch of my aorta.

instead
through their
shielding sunglasses
they see
a wife,
a mother.

i wave back to them.

my sand castle
melts
into the sea.

III: the empress.

i peel oranges
on the beach
for my children.

 they're cutting
slices of wave
with their little bodies,
just like they
cut through me into the artificial
daylight
of the operating room.

spray and giggles drift shoreward,
and the oranges probably
taste like salt now,
as i peel and peel and peel.

sediment.

worried, my son asks me every day
if i know when i am going
to die.

i do envy virginia her
stones, her certainty:

this breath is my last.

then breathless everyone
whispered that from her brilliance
bloomed a rot,

that's the price one pays
for genius,
just ask sylvia.

if you're stupid no one says that,
not if you're dull, just a
mother, most primal of poets.

then it's just selfish whim

as though only firecracker women
deserve bluebonnet ovations—

here and then gone.

IV: the emperor.

he is the sort of man
who buys a zoo ticket
and
claims the right
to pet all of the animals.

then, when he slips his hand
between the wolf's cage bars,
and in a scarlet arc
withdraws
just a nub of gristle and bone,
he screams:

"oh, but she was smiling!"

unsigned.

she watches him put away dinner:
chicken breast, pale and saltless—
he and his family cannot abide
fat or skin or bones—
and challah and purple wine.

"he is a good husband,"
she says, her eyes a bit watery,
her knuckles the same color
as the chicken.

"he treats you like priceless art."

yes, well—

it is a terrible
exhausting
thing,
to be magritte's horse,
useful parts [the head,
the sufficient hips]
on display and the rest
ravaged
by unfeeling trees.

obituary.

i hold my son's hand
as we shelter in the museum
because summer is here
and i sympathize
with the mummies,
with their need for
unrelenting chill.

"that dinosaur has
three horns," he says,
and he chews on his lip
then:

"but we don't know
if he was purple or blue
or maybe rainbow?"

yes, maybe rainbow.

it is a wonder to me
that he can already
see

that just because
the blackened bones
of a thing
sketch a shape,
there are still gaps
where the heart
must have been.

aorta.

no one in texas was
really prepared for the freeze,

for the parabola of polar air
that swept the familiar

off
of its predictable
                    axis.

husband—

i was not
really ready for your gritted teeth,
your winter white knuckles,
the pond ice crack
of the door wood snapping.

do you remember?

when that february's frost
kissed copper pipes,
our water congealed into
an expansive embolism.

then:
when warmth
readjusted the equation
and the icy clots melted,

our plumbing ruptured.
our home flooded.

i am afraid.

i am afraid of you.

i am afraid that if
a woman
ever *really* sees me,
       really smiles at me,
really touches me

the way the sun holds the first wildflowers

i will expand
and burst

and drown.

na'amah.

what burns more brightly:
sunset
or
the chemical flare
blooming over the oil refinery?

it did not rain
like this
when i was a child.

i worried
about books and softball
and protesting too much
when the boy down
the street
called me a dyke.

i did not worry
about leaving an axe
in the attic
just in case
the floodwaters gulped
up the first floor,
then the second.

i brought my sons
into a world
that will need
an ark,

and now i worry
that we bulldozed
all of the olive trees,

now i worry
the dove will learn
rightly from the raven,

now i worry
that there are
no rainbows
left
for them or for me.

VI: the lovers.

the tragedy is:
i convinced myself
i did not need
what
you could not give.

ventricle.

my husband is having an affair

maybe.

i found photos on his phone
of a woman with bright blonde hair
looking, lip bit, at the camera.

his gaze rushed
over and around me
for so long

that the Grand Canyon
makes perfect sense to me,

now.

the slow grinding
violence of it.

a pipe beneath our lawn
started leaking
slowly,

and i might not have noticed
but for the water bill.

six hundred dollars.

well.

then i could see
the depression in the grass,
how the green blades were darker there,
slicked over mud.

bitter herbs.

wildflowers foam against a fractured highway
and frothing
      pool in the swoon
between hills—

you appraise them.
you tell me
      they're beautiful
but
your voice glitters
 like the eyes of a dog
who stole food from
the kitchen table.

winecup paintbrush firewheel bluebonnet:
tame and clumsy titles
        for feral mouths.
i call them all by name,
a small courtesy between
      like minds.

after all, we bloom
for the same reasons,

not for the possessive eye
but to spite the frost and fires
that would
eat us
alive.

haruspex.

science has given us so many things—

my children sliced safe from
my uterus;

vaccines that dull
death's breathtaking crown.

when ancient man first witnessed fire,
i imagine they saw
a divine hand.

now,
we look at the internet
and space travel and our fingerprints
smudge the holiness.

i can't really blame us for needing to see god
to believe in her.

when as a wife and mother
i finally saw
two women kiss

their foreheads pressed together
in sweet and secret prayer—

i realized.

oh.

Oh!

IX: the hermit.

my son holds up his
fist, fingers curled like swans' necks.

"did you know a neutron star is
maybe this small?"

his eyes, excited and luminous,
open moon wide.

"but did you *also* know it is the densest
thing in the universe?"

i did know, yes.

sweet boy, i know—

because except for you and your brother,
except for your supernova
of questions
of hands
of hugs—

i am
a kernel inside of my body,
tiny and impossibly heavy.

supernovas.

i have become a planet
that orbits
my sons.

maybe
some distant day
they will consume me—

balancing Goya.

the queen is in the field.

the hay is baled and baleful,
twisted into hurricane spirals
and left to pasture dry.

between violet flowers
float tissue paper butterflies,
yellow and bright and fragile
unlike
stained glass monarchs.

do they know the world is ending?

no, of course not.

these butterflies
do not stop even for death.

on the last hot gasp of summer
they slip up and over
the windshield crest
of a rusted pickup truck

and flutter
            on
                    unperturbed
as if to say

i have no time for you,

                    can't you see i'm
                            flying?

artemis.

once in a handful of blue moons
snow comes to the hill country,
and when it does:

you'll crumple clothes into canvas bags,
drink your iced coffee as you steer
through sleet   away from the dawn
away from the penetrating arrogance
of sunshine.

> [*after all,*
> *you might never have seen*
> *the rainbows crowding your heart*
> *without the bleak help of*
> *clouds*]

you'll let your children
eat frozen waffles in the backseat
as you chase the winter
exchanging the gulf coast's
broad oak trunks for twisted, thin cedars.

> [*sweet mother, you cannot breathe,*
> *you are overcome with violet longing*
> *for a life and a woman*
> *you might have loved*]

you'll race
hunted and hunting
over the glittering slip of highway

because there is
melting magic
in the way snow crumbles over the golden grass

magic that you need them to see.

binah.

just outside my kitchen window, perched in
the bones of a defiant oak, a red hawk
keens, sharp and insistent and:

> [*breathe, cry, breathe, cry*
> *oh, mother, i need i need i need.*]

that spiral call plants a seed ache in my breasts,
the way my babies sang for milk
the way this hunter sings for meat—

violets blossom belly wide and down
> [*breathe, cry, breathe, cry*
> *oh, yes, i need i need i need.*]
and in the dark of my bed i sing,
alone and dreaming of women
while my husband lurks in the living room.

maybe life and death are not so different,
maybe after winter
all that blooms is
Hunger.

grazing among the lilies.

on the front porch
i fold myself prim into the rocking chair,
    i cradle a butter gilded fried pie in my hands.

does my husband know
that i think of you while i eat—

that i wonder if your flavor
changes with the seasons,
slipping from peach to dusky apple?

do your sighs smell like cinnamon?

no, he doesn't know.
and:

if he sees that my eyes glitter,
he will blame the exuberant cedars
or the melting
decay of the autumn sunset.

pearls.

"a woman of valor, who can find?"

on friday night, he used to sing to me.

i stared at the braided bread
and the candlesticks and
my folded fingers and
wondered why i could not
stuff my heart with white linen
to feel full.

he doesn't sing anymore—he doesn't
have time for that—because it has
nothing to do with
bones.

instead he brings home
grocery store daisies, swooning
in their green plastic dress,
and tosses them on the counter
for me
to clip and tame and curate—

i'm good at that,
at silent flower arrangement,
because my heart is
overgrown with violets
and that's why
he never fit.

"a woman of valor, who can find?"

i found you.

we found each other.

we lived together and
chanted prayers
for and with our friends, every friday—
and then afterward
we would stumble home giggling
to turn on a recording of our
favorite metal band—
and then we would sink into the couch,
together,
laughing a garland of rainbows.

i am so sorry i was colorblind,
then.

there we were—
and then we weren't.

like one of your pomegranates
we cracked apart, bleeding
sweet,
and we circled our husbands
under separate
wedding canopies.

when i light candles now,
in the quiet after my children
are soothed to sleep,

i wonder
if you still knead
honey and salt into your challah,
if you still like wine that smells
like cherries and turns your lips purple,

if we could have circled each other
if i had known.

inquisition.

you're damn right,
i'm a witch.

we can start there
and skip the trial.

let's not waste
my time.

yes:

i worship
the oak tree and the moon,
the fox and the stag,
the bluebonnets and the secret violets.

they have never asked me
to be anything other than
wild.

yes:

sometimes if you're lucky
you might catch me dancing
unclothed in my kitchen.

my thighs have supported
me through worse
than this.

yes:

i tuck paper amulets
into my children's
armored backpacks.

but i think we both know
that if men possessed
any magic at all,
you'd do the same thing.

and yes, i am guilty
of the deepest witchcraft:

i spoke aloud the true name
of the man who
violated
me
and every ward
a woman holds dear.

i
    told

           everyone.

now:

i am so tired, please
burn me alive.

chesed.

i will die one day and when
i do, the rainbows no longer contained
by my ribs and sealed mouth
will leak—

i can think of a dozen people who, offended,
will gasp, maybe even weep, and grieve
for that secret they were not trusted
to keep,

but: will they think on
the spotted fawn,
why she trembles in the long grass

and from whose teeth
she   is hiding?

cauldron.

grandmother cast iron is the best
everyone knows that but i don't have any
hers rusted in one of the hurricanes
i can't remember which one,

i lost track of my storms.

    so

i make do with a new pan i try my best
even though the grip is love unsmoothed
and it gets too hot too fast
and it refuses to hold seasoning
and it snaps at raw meat and holds
for
        dear life.

maybe after eighteen years of
my rainbowed fingers my tallowed palms
maybe one
           night

the wet will take
settle into the metal
weed any lingering rust flowers
leaving only violet black.

can't say i blame the iron, though—
can't say that i do.

i know what it is to want something so badly
that you're willing to
burn.

glut.

i drive my children
to school, each and every morning;
sometimes against the bayou gray
an osprey skims.

"is that a vulture?"
my older son asks,
his forehead pressed against
glass stained artificially dark.

i forgive him his confusion;

most people here
                    can't see
the difference between a vulture—
a hovering, hovering,
black question mark—

                    [is that squirrel cracked open,
                    skeleton egg, circled upon itself
                    in dry winter grass
                    or is it asleep?]

and the osprey, all decisive angles.

what a miracle,

                    what an enviable magic

to dive into water
coagulated with oil and mud

to slip clean away
wet and alive,

to glut
on a rainbow.

phosphorous.

peonies should be fed in early spring
and then, again, after they bloom;

synthesized fertilizers aren't
suitably nourishing—
for healthy buds you need
blood meal and bone meal.

my brain folds in on itself
as a spiral of slippery petals—
the secret rot is at my center
where no one can find it.

oh, my darlings,
my sweet boys—

i am no master gardener,
i have no one to teach me,

but i will grind my skeleton
to dust
and empty my ventricles
for you

if it means
you will grow
wildly whole

where i did not.

filly.

texan summer is technicolor—

if the pines aren't burning,
if there is sweet sufficient rain.

no emerald can outshine the grass,
or the glittering golden horses
flashing against blue clouds
dark with sponged up sky.

               is it *bright* like this,
where you are?

does ocean salt work
through your heart
the way it does in food—
does it sharpen your appetite
for me?

mare.

galveston bay isn't anything like
the aegean, all sapphires and wine

   but: if

i close my eyes halfway
i can trace your
                  throat's temple arch
in the curling foam.

maybe thrace and texas
aren't so different—

great hercules fed human hearts
to a hungry herd, and every cowboy
will tell you that
his best mare is also

   violent.

in my oil slick oracle i scry a
      rainbow truth:

they're afraid of us, love,
ancient greeks and modern men, they know

i would take
            you between
      my teeth
like sweetgrass

and then i might stay wild,
              mane violet and bluebonnet
crowned—

and then no man could break

me.

cirrus.

clouds sweep curls across
the moon's
pale perfect jaw

and i know
i could be
that gentle
with you

if you would let me.

but you go home.
to your husband.

i will go home to mine,
but not before

i ask the coyotes
to scream hymns
on my behalf.

kaddish.

what's the difference between singing
and screaming, anyway?

or singing, and screaming, and sighing—

it's a question of air, i think;
otherwise the motions are the same.

i learned in choir to keep my jaw
slack and round, stressless
for clear music.

your fingers pull the same
notes from my throat:
a thread of pearls
i thought i lost
at sea.

as for screaming:

i am a mother,
i have seen red photos from bucha,
from palestine and israel,
from the elementary school down the highway.

silver.

people are fascinated
by women
who change their shape.

fox, seal, mare, wolf:

i don't know that
the form matters so much—

they only care
that we look human to their eyes,
feel familiar under their fingers,

and then we do not.

we trade the chorion curl
of hipbones and breasts
for fur and fang and freedom.

we hunt half mad, holy wild

under
the light of the moon.

> [*in all the songs, it is always*
> *the full moon that changes us,*
> *though She is no less powerful*
> *when She is hidden.*]

oh, my sisters
of sky and sea and shadow.

i can howl my heart's envy
because no one is listening,
because no one whispers stories
about those of us who linger

bone bound
by precious bodies,
by tender palms,
by a mother's promise

[*i think the moon understands, though,*
i think She forgives me for staying
just a little longer, a little longer].

tiferet.

i would love you the way
small bats fly in spring,

not with the hawk's aggressive air,
nor the osprey's certain slice,

just cupping wind gently
a grateful, steady softness—
thank you
thank you
thank you.

lenticular.

my horse

thought to taste
my shirt but
with his sleepy eyes
and heavy jaws

      he bit too deeply.

and now
violets bloom
in the cleft of my ribs

and i love love love
that perfect secret ache.

your husband is away,
out on some vacation or business trip—

      my husband notices nothing.

so you *can* call me,
and you *do*,

      oh, you do.

and we talk and we laugh
and i splay my palm against
my bruise,

i push, just a little,
at the tender dark

whenever i make you laugh.

hod.

what a wonder the way my mind slips
different prisms against what i see,
and hear, and taste—

when i walk the woods with my children,
we see fallen logs as balance beams—
the footprints of armadillos and possums
as play paths to trace.

but when i am here alone—

all that i can see is you

> [*you are everywhere, always,*
> *silent spring*
> > *between the sheets i share with my husband*]

in the seed fluff, cream colored,   caught
between hairs of curling grass,

in the burnt black oak
haunted by the memory of rain,

in the yaupon berries that soak up
the sun's golden touch and turn the light
pink and translucent and sweet

for grateful does to devour.

the world stands upon three things.

it was my fault
that the dog and i
had to shelter under
one of the neighborhood
oaks.

i forgot that here on the gulf coast
thunderstorms bloom
hot and fast
as wildfire.

but still in the trembling grass
robins hop

                rose-breasted and wet.

they watch me,
they watch my dog,

then the birds return
to worrying the earth for worms

because
even if it's raining

                you should not forget to eat.

velvet shed.

he asks me: do i have any fantasies.

i suddenly understand
the glazed opal eyes
of a crownless doe,
headlight haloed before,

    well.

at least it was brief.

he wasn't actually looking for
    me:
he only wanted
the sun turned on
himself.

but you, my love, there is
    nothing
 swift about you, nothing
    certain.

lipstick smooth,
you call me a wild thing,
made luminous by
my
    undone
        antlered
            hair.

i do have a question—
(just one, though,
only if i am allowed)

what do you see when you look at me:

    a bright and guiding constellation,
        or the soft empty between stars?

yesod.

a rainbow is a promise,
that's what they taught my children
at day school, and then they sent
them home with challahs
dyed every artificial color.

a promise, yes. also
an apology,

no different from when i—
    tired of being alone in a marriage,
    of a hurricane season that stretches for ten years in either direction—
lose my temper
over something stupid like
not eating enough chicken nuggets
or not making a bed.

i try to say that i'm sorry, quick if i can,
lightning quick:
i'm so sorry,
and i promise
to try harder
to be better,

then
i take them for ice cream with
rainbow sprinkles.

aspic.

shabbat is coming
luminous bride with her pearls
her pomegranates

my heart cracks open
and a raven slips out
trailing a
                veil of violets.

shopping   for brisket and flowers,
close to the rose buckets
i see two
        women
whispering to each other:
secret grocery lists, maybe,
or
        the psalmist's most earthly
                    promises.

they kiss
and i
        shove
my hand
into the roses' thorny thick.

i shove the
                        meat of my want
down
down

down.

i suspend

myself

in a slick and jellied chill.

honey butter.

a dangerous game to slide your fingers
through me while i try and fail to focus on:

frying latkes and doughnuts, circles in gasping oil,
the curl of your hand between my thighs,
the bubble of my (o p e n m o u t h).

you whisper something stupid sweet about
seasoning, about how i need to be seasoned,
rainbow greased,
and i laugh at the iron
truth of it—

having rusted in neglect for so, so long
that everything sticks to me
Everything.

sacred geology.

how do you cut your biscuit?

i think
that proper people
slice along a horizontal axis—
that's better for peach jam and butter

but i
cleave straight down the middle

so i
can see the air that tried to escape—
a captured gasp
is delicious,
isn't it?

holiness builds a fence for itself.

our mystics animated
a gelatinous clay figure—

> *probably red, or maybe horse white,*
> *this earth marrow—*

by scabbing the hebrew word
for [truth]
across its bramble blooming forehead.

> *a new century demands a new commandment:*
> *in strength there is safety.*

then,
before a quartz-boned
and mud-muscled

[Golem]

the pressing bloody urgency
melted away,
> *a limp and pallid fog.*
So

no need now for a living ward,
no need now for shambling magic,

those mystics
smeared one letter into
incomprehension

sparing the word for
[death.]

are death and truth siblings
separated only by a slender scrawl,
                        or is anything other than
                                        honesty a kind of dying?

is my detailed exegesis
of little, shuddering deaths
endured under the weight of proud men

                a venomous fiction?

i need
a woman's hands to pluck
at the prism of my aorta—

it will take a woman's hands
to animate my heart,

                        i think.

II: the high priestess.

when my husband touches me
i close my eyes

the better to summon
my golem
sculpted of a thousand women
i wish i had bravely loved.

and yet, and yet, and yet:
with every little death
i *live* a little more.

glossal.

summer now and the grass is silver
and gold in a dry and angry way
that frightens people,

hay already before any cutting or bale twine,
hill after hill fire fertile,
black only where flames have bloomed—

i have not tasted manna
but i know what it smells like,
a wet and glittering grace

that unspools when the grass
greens under thunder's thumb,

stretches up to rainbows
hidden behind blue clouds

as if that is all the earth
ever needed.

XVII: the star.

spring is here and the green grass
draws deer down to the dawn highway,
does and antlered stags all alike
in Death, bones scattered as
a graveled tracery of clouds

while overhead on warm wide wings
between white ribs a dozen hot hearts
spiral
spiral
spiral

down

over black branches that pink
under sunlight fingers

and maybe i'll never tell you that
i love you,
maybe i'll die with the words
on my tongue
and let a vulture carry them

up.

architect.

loose, laceless i lean over you
laughing and laughing i look
like the famous she-wolf and you

lick your lips, ask me:
what cities could we have built
together
if we hadn't married

men?

tzedek: the wild hunt.

listen, more than a few witches have seen
Leviathan; he's hard to miss
if you know what you're looking for,
all oil-slick sinew and chemical eyes—

whispered rumor is that he
favors the gulf because the water isn't clear,
no good for scrying being bayou fed,

and oil rigs make men believe they are
nephilim, invincible as david until
they meet him and his electric teeth.

Behemoth is also well-known,
her green and looping power tendril taut
all through and up the muscled appalachians,
down to the wildflower prairies.

i have called on her strength twice:
once to protect my body,
once to protect my children,

from the same man.

don't worry, he won't bother us again
he knows now that i am not some
texas limestone golem born
to crumble under salt and tears . . .

oh, but you don't want to hear about that,
no one ever does.

the Ziz, you asked about the Ziz.

well.

the Ziz is so rare that
our rabbis and mystics say
they do not exist
except in wild
dreams.

mothers with secrets know better.
i know better.

i saw it on an x-ray of my spine,
while my doctors focused on
rebelling vertebrae—

a soft egg dark beside bright bones,
nestled up against my liver.

the Ziz feeds on my heart, you see,
it nests in a tangle of veined violets
and women i love when no one
is looking.

and one day when i am safe,
when my children are safe
the Ziz will hatch,

feathers will bloom
from my mouth and
on covenant-colored wings

i will
just
fly
away.

malkhut.

how unlike the ocean
  i am—
i have no
depths that i hide from you.

but when you are
full flashing silver,
  i feel
a growing, greater swell.

and when you fold yourself
into the dark,
i smooth out my
hurricane waves and wait.

  didn't you know?

everything holy is a circle,
in the end.

NOTES

KETER

Hebrew for "crown;" also the topmost of the Kabbalistic concepts known as *sefirot*.

AVINU MALKEINU, 5781

Literally "Our Father, Our King." Avinu Malkeinu is a Jewish prayer recited on Rosh Hashanah, the New Year, and through the ten days leading up to Yom Kippur, the Day of Atonement.

BINAH

Hebrew for "understanding," binah is the third of the Kabbalistic *sefirot*.

PEARLS

"A woman of valor," also known in Hebrew as *Aishes Chayil*, is a portion of the Book of Proverbs that describes what is considered an upright, righteous woman.

CHESED

Hebrew for "kindness or love between people;" chesed is also one of the Kabbalistic *sefirot*.

KADDISH

The Kaddish, in one of its forms, is a traditional Jewish mourner's prayer and is not traditionally recited without the presence of other people.

TIFERET

Hebrew for "glory or splendor," tiferet is one of the Kabbalistic *sefirot*.

HOD

Hebrew for "majesty," hod is one of the Kabbalistic *sefirot*.

YESOD

Hebrew for "foundation," yesod is one of the bottom *sefirot* in the Kabbalah.

TZEDEK: THE WILD HUNT

Hebrew for "justice," and most commonly associated with the phrase "Tzedek, tzedek tirdof!" which translates as "Justice, justice you shall pursue!"

MALKHUT

Hebrew for "kingdom," and the base or bottom of the *sefirot* in Kabbalah.

ABOUT THE ARTWORK:

Samuel Jessurun de Mesquita (1868–1944) was an early twentieth-century Dutch Jewish artist. During World War II, he was taken to Auschwitz with his wife and killed in the gas chambers.

Interior images: (All via rawpixel. Originals from The Rijksmuseum.)
  p. 12: *Giant heron (Reuzenreiger)* (1915).
  p. 22: *Vrouwelijk naakt achter vaas met aronskelken* (1912).
  p. 33: *Cows (Koeien)* (1916).
  p. 53: *Sunflower (Zonnebloem)* (1914).
  p. 62: *The music (De muziek)* (1878–1943).

ACKNOWLEDGMENTS

Some of the poems included in *Spellbook for the Sabbath Queen* have been previously printed in various literary magazines, and I appreciate these publications for giving my poems their first glimpse of sunlight.

"selkie." in *Sand Hills Literary Magazine*

"kelp." in *Change Seven*

"marrow." and "na'amah." in *Sheila-Na-Gig*

"unsigned." in *Berru* and then *Paper Brigade*, both published by the Jewish Book Council

"obituary." in *Heartwood Literary Magazine* (semifinalist for the Heartwood Poetry Prize)

"aorta." and "ventricle." in *Rhino Poetry* (finalists for their Founders' Prize)

"bitter herbs." in *The McNeese Review*

"IX: the hermit." in *Cordella Magazine*

"artemis." and "cirrus." in Allegory Ridge's third volume of their poetry anthology, *Aurora*

"grazing among the lilies." in *The Festival Review*

"pearls." in *805 Lit + Art* (nominee for Best of the Net)

"cauldron." in Belle Point Press's *Mid/South Anthology*

"glut." in *Welter*

"phosphorous." and "mare." in the second volume of *Brazos River Review*

"filly." in *Susurrus*

"silver." in *Penumbra Online*

"lenticular." in the first volume of *Brazos River Review*

"the world stands upon three things." in *Olney Magazine*

"aspic." in *Passengers Journal*

"honey butter." in *Moist: The Kink Issue*

"holiness builds a fence for itself." in *the gamut mag*

"XVII: the star." in *Rust + Moth*

"tzedek: the wild hunt." in *Strange Horizons*

I cannot adequately express my gratitude to Casie Dodd for believing in this work and giving it a home. I am grateful to Becca Kantor, as well, for publishing my first poem and taking a chance on me.

I would also like to thank A.W. for her ceaseless encouragement and critical eye; H.A. for color-sorted markers and strength; M.C. and H.R. for their magical support; R.B. for live oak lunches; and N.H. for embodying everything an *aishes chayil* should be and then some.

And most importantly: my sun + my moon—I hope one day you understand how vitally I love y'all.

ELISHEVA FOX is a poet with roots firmly planted in Texan soil. A finalist for the Gwendolyn Brooks Poetry Prize, she has also been nominated for Best of the Net. Her work has appeared in *Rust + Moth*, *Paper Brigade*, *Strange Horizons*, and *Sand Hills Literary Magazine*, among others. This is her first collection of poems.

Printed in the USA
CPSIA information can be obtained
at www.ICGtesting.com
LVHW041926261123
764961LV00010B/244